CLEAN E

presents

JOANNE

by
**Deborah Bruce, Theresa Ikoko,
Laura Lomas, Chino Odimba
and Ursula Rani Sarma**

First performed at Latitude Festival on 19 July 2015
and Soho Theatre on 13 October 2015

JOANNE

by Deborah Bruce, Theresa Ikoko,
Laura Lomas, Chino Odimba
and Ursula Rani Sarma

CAST

Tanya Moodie

CREATIVE TEAM

DIRECTOR	**Róisín McBrinn**
DESIGNER	**Lucy Osborne**
LIGHTING DESIGNER	**Emma Chapman**
SOUND DESIGNER	**Becky Smith**
ASSISTANT DIRECTOR	**Laura Asare**

Clean Break would like to acknowledge the generous support of all its funders and supporters with special thanks to Arts Council England, John Ellerman Foundation, Esmée Fairbairn Foundation, and NoraLee & Jon Sedmak for supporting *Joanne*.

Introduction

We commissioned *Joanne* in early 2015 to be performed at Latitude Festival. At that time, the run-up to the General Election was underway and there was media saturation of rhetoric around cuts, cuts, cuts. We were offering additional and emergency support services at Clean Break (including emergency housing clinics and food-bank vouchers) in order to compensate for pressure on almost all the essential external services that are used by women attending our theatre-education programme. In addition, the backdrop to these pressures was reduced access to legal aid and a probation service undergoing privatisation. I began to see the women employees who are the 'faces' of our public services as the front line of a very brittle army, kept fighting through good will and human endurance. Inspired by this, I wanted to create a piece of theatre that looks at the fallout of this continuing unsustainable system – to look at the pressure on the front line and where it actually implodes. Joanne is the invisible fall out. Through the pressures on public services, the person that arguably needs these resources the most, gets lost and in some way disappears.

Joanne is a young woman, who shares her story with the women we work with day in day out at Clean Break and in women's prisons. The challenge of the production was to create something that purposefully excluded Joanne's voice whilst also ensuring that this was a virtue and not a loss. We worked with Clean Break's Student Support Team to create a timeline for our 'Jo Bloggs'. It was important that there were multiple times in her young trajectory that Joanne could have been helped with the right intervention, and that this woman's *pathway* to prison and beyond was one that could have been diverted. I then worked with our five commissioned writers to explore the central twenty-four hours that the play focuses on and to consider the women that Joanne comes into contact with. Our writers – Deborah, Theresa, Laura, Ursula and Chino – then went and spoke to women who work in their chosen characters' professions. It was important that each writer had an autonomous voice in the process whilst also trying to ensure the five pieces hung together and became fuller as a whole.

Having Deborah, Theresa, Ursula, Laura and Chino working on this project was a real thrill for the company. Not only are they each writers that Clean Break admires hugely, it was also wonderful to gain so many different insights into a single arena and event. Part of the aim of the project was to explore the diversity of lives and pressures on service-led women's employment. Inviting Tanya Moodie to join this cohort of stellar female artists seemed a natural progression. She has extended each of these voices with her wonderful collaborative spirit and great talent and hopefully left Joanne's absence very present for you at a time when she urgently needs to be visible.

Róisín McBrinn
Director, *Joanne*
Head of Artistic Programme, Clean Break

Cast and Creative Team

Deborah Bruce (Writer)
Credits include: *Godchild* (Hampstead Theatre, 2013); *Same* (NT Connections, 2013); *The Distance* (Orange Tree Theatre, 2014; Sheffield Crucible, 2015).

Theresa Ikoko (Writer)
Credits include: *Visiting Hours* (Belgrade Theatre, 2014); *Normal* (Talawa Firsts, 2014; HighTide Festival, 2015).

Laura Lomas (Writer)
Laura is currently Channel 4 Resident Playwright at Clean Break. Recent work includes *Ask* (Royal Court/ ICT); *Bird* (Root Theatre/ tour); *Blister* (Paines Plough); *Glue* (E4). She is currently under commission to Clean Break, Manchester Royal Exchange, Royal Court Theatre and Nottingham Playhouse.

Chino Odimba (Writer)
Chino is currently under commission to Clean Break for a new play to be produced in 2016. Credits include: *A Blues for Nia* (Eclipse Theatre/BBC); *His name is Ishmael* (Bristol Old Vic, 2013); *The Birdwoman of Lewisham* (Arcola, 2015).

Ursula Rami Sarma (Writer)
Credits include: *Yerma* (West Yorkshire Playhouse, 2011); *Birdsong* (Abbey Theatre Dublin, 2010); *The Dark Things* (Traverse Theatre, 2009); *The Spidermen* (National Theatre, 2007).

Tanya Moodie (Stella/Grace/Kathleen/Alice/Becky)
Tanya trained at RADA. Her many stage roles have included Rose in *Fences* opposite Lenny Henry in the West End, for which she was nominated for Best Actress in the 2014 What's On Stage Awards. For her performance as Esther in *Intimate Apparel* at the Park Theatre, she was nominated for Best Actress at the 2014 London Evening Standard Theatre Awards, as well as an Olivier 2015 nomination for Outstanding Achievement in an Affiliate Theatre. That same year she was also nominated for an Olivier for Outstanding Achievement in an Affiliate Theatre for her performance as Makeda in *The House That Will Not Stand* at the Tricycle Theatre. Television includes the role of Ella in two series of *Sherlock*.

Róisín McBrinn (Director)
Róisín is Head of Artistic Programme at Clean Break. *Joanne* is her first production for the company. She has directed productions for some of the UK and Ireland's most important theatres including: *Afterplay* by Brian Friel (Sheffield Crucible); *Yerma* by Lorca in a version by Ursula Rani Sarma (West Yorkshire Playhouse); *No Escape* by Mary Raftery, *Perve* by Stacey Gregg, *Heartbreak House* by GB Shaw (Abbey Theatre); *66 Books* (Bush Theatre). She has developed new plays for the Traverse Theatre, Bush Theatre, National Theatre, Soho Theatre,

Abbey Theatre and Manchester Royal Exchange. She was Associate Director at Sherman Cymru until 2013. While she was there she directed *Before It Rains* by Katherine Chandler (co-production with Bristol Old Vic), *The Sleeping Beauties* and *Peter Pan* by Robert Alan Evans, *The Get Together* and *It's A Family Affair* by Simon Crowther, as well as leading the nurturing and development of Welsh and Wales-based new writing for the company. Róisín was the inaugural recipient of the Quercus Award 2010 run by the National Theatre and was resident at the National Theatre Studio in 2009. In 2004 she won the Young Vic/Jerwood Young Director's Award.

Lucy Osborne (Designer)
Lucy's theatre designs include: *Luna Gale, Hello Goodbye, In the Vale of Health, Blue Heart Afternoon* (Hampstead); *Privacy, Coriolanus, Berenice, The Recruiting Officer* (Donmar Warehouse); *Translations, Plenty, The Unthinkable, The Long and the Short and the Tall* (Sheffield Theatres); *Lampedusa* (Soho and HighTide Festival); *The Machine* (Manchester International Festival/NYC); *Huis Clos* (Donmar Trafalgar Season); *Twelfth Night* (Winner of the Chicago Jeff Award for Scenic Design); *The Taming of the Shrew* (Chicago Shakespeare Theatre); *Shades* (Royal Court); *Utopia* (Live, Newcastle/Soho); *X & Y* (Complicite/Science Museum); *Precious Little Talent* (Trafalgar Studios). Lucy is the co-designer of Roundabout, a portable theatre, which won The Stage Awards Theatre Building of the Year 2015. Her work for Paines Plough includes *Lungs, The Initiate, Our Teacher's a Troll, The Angry Brigade* (also Bush Theatre); *An Intervention* (Watford Palace/UK tour); *Jumpers For Goalposts* (Hull Truck, Watford Palace and Bush Theatre); *Love, Love, Love* (Royal Court/National Tour).

Emma Chapman (Lighting Designer)
Emma Chapman trained at Bristol Old Vic Theatre School. With Lucy Osborne and Howard Eaton, Emma Chapman designed The Stage Awards' Theatre Building of the Year 2015: Roundabout, commissioned by Paines Plough. Theatre credits include: *Boi Boi is Dead* (Watford Palace Theatre and West Yorkshire Playhouse co-production); *The Human Ear; Lungs; The Initiate, Our Teacher's a Troll* (Roundabout, Paines Plough); *Rose* (Edinburgh); *The Planet and Stuff, Run, The Machine Gunners* (Polka Theatre); *Dublin Carol* (Donmar season); *Sex with a Stranger* (Trafalgar Studios); *The Sea Plays* (Old Vic Tunnels); *Donkey's Years* (Rose Theatre, Kingston); *Mules, You Can See the Hills, Parallel Hamlet* (Young Vic); *Bus Stop* (New Vic, Stoke/Stephen Joseph Theatre); *Dangerous Corner, Dick Whittington* (Theatre Royal, Bury St Edmunds); *Lulu* (Gate). Opera credits include: *Il turco in Italia* (Angers/Nantes Opera Luxembourg); *Xerxes, Carmen* (Royal Northern College of Music, Manchester); *Così fan tutte* (Royal College of Music); *The Pied Piper* (Opera North). She has also lit *Rumplestiltskin* for London Children's Ballet at the Peacock Theatre, available on DVD. Other notable engagements include Olivier Award-winning play *The Mountaintop* (Theatre503/Trafalgar Studio); *The Painter*, which opened the new Arcola Theatre; *Wet Weather Cover* (King's Head/Arts Theatre).

Becky Smith (Sound Designer)
Becky studied drama at Exeter University. Her sound designs for Clean Break include: *Little on the inside* (Summerhall, Edinburgh); *Billy the Girl*, *This Wide Night* (Soho Theatre): *it felt empty when the heart went at first but it is alright now* (Arcola Theatre); *A Just Act* (prison tour); *Missing Out* (prison tour). Other sound designs include: *36 Phonecalls* (Hampstead Theatre Downstairs); *The Day After* (Vault Festival); *Bird* (Derby Playhouse); *Circles* (Birmingham Rep); *Frozen* (Birmingham Rep); *The Only Way Is Chelsea's* (York Theatre Royal); *The Kitchen Sink* (Hull Truck); *The Well and the Badly Loved*, *Lagan* (Ovalhouse); *Cardboard Dad* (Sherman Cymru); *Brood* (Stratford East); *The Juniper Tree* (UK tour); *Reverence* (Southwark Playhouse); *The Ghost Sonata* (Trinity Buoy Wharf). Becky also freelances in Radio Drama for the BBC.

Caitlin O'Reilly (Stage Manager)
Caitlin is a freelance events/productions professional and has been working as a stage manager for the past five years. For the past year she has been working on *The 39 Steps* (Criterion Theatre). Other work includes: *Napoleon Blown Apart*, *Boy*, *PlayWROUGHT*, *Misbehaving*, *The Insect Play*, *Used Car Junkyard* (Arcola Theatre); *As You Like It* (Southwark Playhouse). As well as site-specific work with *Nonsuch Theatre* as part of Nottingham's *Light Night*. Her next project will be with *Ben Hur* (Tricycle Theatre). She has been production managing for *Cultivated Nonsense*, *Gypsy Disco* at festivals and venues all over the UK. Other events include *Greenwich Comedy Festival*, *Bristol Comedy Garden* and *Lost & Found - Interactive Nonsense Facilitators.*

Ali Beale (Production Manager)
Theatre includes: *You For Me For You*, *Plaques and Tangles*, *Who Cares* (Royal Court); *Men & Girls Dance*, *Little Universe*, *Dusk*, *Above Me the Wide Blue Sky*, *It's the Skin You're Living In*, *The Forest*, *Brilliant*, *Stilled*, *An Infinite Line Brighton*, *And the Rain Falls Down*, *The Summer Subversive*, *Fleet*, *The Field of Miracles*, *Feat Your Eyes* (& co-designer; Fevered Sleep); *Sweatbox*, *Pests*, *Re-Charged*, *Just Act*, *it felt empty when the heart went at first but it is alright now*, *Missing Out*, *This Wide Night*, *Black Crows* (Clean Break); *Under Glass*, *Must*, *Performing Medicine*, *Sampled*, *Fantastic Voyage* (The Clod Ensemble); Give Us a Hand! (The Little Angel); *The Contents of a House*, *Guided Tour* (Peter Reder); *The Evocation of Papa Mas*, *The Firework Maker's Daughter*, *Aladdin*, *Playing the Victim*, *A Little Fantasy*, *Shoot Me in the Heart* (Told by An Idiot); *Gumbo Jumbo* (The Gogmagogs); *The Ratcatcher of Hamlin* (Cartoon De Salvo); *Oogly Boogly* (Tom Morris/Guy Dartnell); *Throat* (Company FZ); *Arcane* (Opera Circus). Film includes: *Dusk*, *It's the Skin You're Living In*, *Still Life with Dog* (Fevered Sleep). Work with artists includes: *Spotlight*, *Backdrop 1*, *Backdrop 2* (Lucy Joyce, Blue Skies Commission).

For *Joanne*

Production Team
Senior Producer **Helen Pringle**
Producer **Kirstin Shirling**
Company Stage Manager **Caitlin O'Reilly**
Production Manager **Ali Beale**

Marketing and Press
Marketing Consultants **The Cogency**
Press Consultant **Nancy Poole PR**

Clean Break Executive Director
Lucy Perman MBE

Thanks
Our thanks go to Kathy Burke, Anna Gaunt, Kathleen
Richardson, Tanya Tighe, Diana Mumbi, Ony Uhiara and
those in frontline services who talked to our writers as
they conducted their research.

Cover Artist: Ed Fairburn

*This text went to press before the end of rehearsals and so may
differ slightly from the play as performed.*

CLEAN BREAK

Acclaimed theatre company Clean Break produces ground-breaking plays with women writers and actors at the heart of its work. Founded in 1979 by two women prisoners who needed urgently to tell their stories through theatre, the company today has an independent education programme delivering theatre opportunities to women offenders and women at risk, in custodial and community settings. Clean Break's innovative education work, combined with visionary expertise in theatre, makes for a powerful mix. Celebrated by critics and audience across the UK, the company's award winning plays hit a collective nerve, humanising some of the most difficult things we need to talk about as a society.

Recent productions include: Vivienne Franzmann's *Pests* (Royal Exchange Theatre/Royal Court Theatre co-production and touring); Katie Hims' *Billy the Girl* (Soho Theatre and prison tour); Suhayla El-Bushra's *Fingertips* (Latitude); Alice Birch's *Little on the inside* (Almeida, Latitude and Edinburgh); Rebecca Prichard's *Dream Pill* (Almeida, Edinburgh and touring); *There Are Mountains* by Chloë Moss (HMP & YOI Askham Grange); *RE-Charged*, three plays by Sam Holcroft, Rebecca Lenkiewicz, Chloë Moss (Soho Theatre London 2011); *Charged*, a season of six plays by E V Crowe, Sam Holcroft, Rebecca Lenkiewicz, Chloë Moss, Winsome Pinnock& Rebecca Prichard (Soho Theatre 2010); *it felt empty when the heart went at first but it is alright now* by Lucy Kirkwood (Arcola Theatre, joint winner of the John Whiting Award 2010); and This Wide Night by Chloë Moss (Soho Theatre 2008 and revived in 2009, winner of the Susan Smith Blackburn Award 2009).

Productions from our Graduate Students include: *Sweatbox* by Chloë Moss (Latitude and currently touring); *Meal Ticket* devised in collaboration with Forced Entertainment (Latitude); *Frientimacy* by Stacey Gregg (Donmar Studios); *Sounds Like An Insult* by Vivienne Franzmann (tour); *This is Where We're From* by Morgan Lloyd Malcolm (Clean Break Studios); *Stepping Off the Edge of the World* by Roz Wyllie (tour); and *Hours til' Midnight* by Sonya Hale (tour).

Changing lives and changing minds appeal – help us make a difference

'I've seen the impact of Clean Break's work – both on the women it works with in prisons and students on its London education programme, and on audiences in theatres across the country. It is an organisation that changes lives and changes minds.'
Dame Harriet Walter DBE, Actor and Clean Break Patron

Most of the 3,900 women in prison each year are serving sentences for non-violent crime, often linked to poor mental health, addiction, poverty, racism and lack of education. The majority are themselves victims of crime and due to their frequent caring responsibilities and high support needs, their offending has a disproportionate social and economic impact. Empowering these women to overcome the often significant challenges they face can therefore transform not only their lives but our society.

There is no other organisation like Clean Break in the UK. For 36 years we have continuously made a difference to the lives of women offenders and today, we are widely recognised as a sector leader in criminal justice, women's development and the cultural industries.

Your support will help Clean Break make a difference:

- engaging audiences and creating debate through bold new plays by the UK's most exciting women playwrights addressing the theme of women, crime and justice;
- building confidence, skills and qualifications for women in prison, former offenders and women at risk of offending;
- professional development for criminal justice staff, using short productions, training and discussion to deepen understanding and reconnect professionals with women's experiences.

As a registered charity, our work is only possible thanks to support from individuals and organisations who share our commitment to transforming the lives of vulnerable women affected by the criminal justice system. Donations can be made by sending a cheque by post, online at www.cleanbreak.org.uk or by texting 'CBT14' followed by your chosen amount (for example 'CBT14 £10') to 70070. Every donation will make a lasting difference. If you would like to find out more about supporting Clean Break, please contact Elizabeth Banner, Development Adviser on 020 7482 8608 or liz.banner@cleanbreak.org.uk.

For Clean Break

Executive Director   **Lucy Perman MBE**
Head of Finance and Senior Producer   **Helen Pringle**
Head of Artistic Programme   **Róisín McBrinn**
Head of Education   **Anna Herrmann**
Head of Engagement   **Imogen Ashby**
Assistant Head of Education (Learning)   **Vishni Velada-Billson**
Assistant Head of Education (Student Services)   **Jacqueline Stewart**
Interim General Manager   **Jane McMorrow**
Producer   **Kirstin Shirling**
Theatre Education Manager   **Laura McCluskey**
Theatre Education Manager   **Lorraine Faissal**
Student Support Worker   **Grace Adejuwon**
Student Support Worker   **Carole Jarvis**
Outreach Worker   **Lauren Sammé**
Digital Artist in Residence   **Natasha McDonnell**
Volunteer Coordinator   **Samantha McNeil**
Senior Development Manager   **Lillian Ashford**
Development Manager   **Emily Goodyer**
Finance Manager   **Laura Mallows**
Office Administrator   **Lucy Grant**
Administrative Assistant   **Jeanette Robinson**
Education Administrator   **Verity LaRoche**
Cleaner   **Pauline Bernard**

Board of Directors
Kim Evans OBE (Chair), Suzanne Bell, Jude Boyles, Deborah
Coles, Doreen Foster, Lucy Kirkwood, Alice Millest, Sonali Naik,
Kate Paradine, Susan J Royce, Tanya Tracey, Despina Tsatsas,
Denise White

Patrons
Lord Paul Boateng, Carmen Callil, Dame Judi Dench DBE, Sir
Richard Eyre CBE, Barbara Hosking CBE, Baroness Helena
Kennedy QC, Kevin McGrath, Ann Mitchell, Yve Newbold LLB,
Baroness Usha Prashar CBE, Dr Joan Scanlon JP, Baroness Vivien
Stern CBE, Dame Janet Suzman DBE, Emma Thompson, Dame
Harriet Walter DBE, Lia Williams

Clean Break
2 Patshull Road
London
NW5 2LB
Registered company number 2690758
Registered charity number 1017560

Tel: 020 7482 8600
Fax: 020 7482 8611
general@cleanbreak.org.uk
www.cleanbreak.org.uk
facebook.com/cleanbreak
@CleanBrk

Clean Break would like to acknowledge the generous support of all its
funders and supporters. Clean Break is a member of ITC.

STELLA

Chino Odimba

Character

STELLA, *a woman in her late forties*

Setting

An office

Note on the Text

An ellipsis (…) indicates a trailing-off or pause at the end of dialogue

A forward slash (/) indicates an overlap in speech

STELLA *is leaning against a table.*

The table is full of boxes and plants and bits.

STELLA *is holding a paper party cup.*

Wine in the office eh? That's a treat. I mean it is five-thirty and well I don't have to worry about getting the sack do I?

(*Short beat.*)

I'm not really in to speeches but if it'll shut you up here goes…

(STELLA *hitches herself onto the table.*)

…This is how they do it in the films isn't it? I mean I could 'ave been a film star. You should have seen me at eighteen. Legs up to here.

(STELLA *giggles.*
STELLA *strikes a pose.*)

Anyway I really want to say thanks so much for being the best people to work with. Well most of you eh! My project funding has run out and I'm out on my ear but…

(STELLA *walks the length of the table.*)

…I mean don't get me wrong. If it wasn't for this job. If it wasn't for them believing in me. Anyway you know what I mean. Not many options to put my – (*Gestures quotation marks with her fingers.*) experience to good use if you know what I mean. Not many options at that time anyway…

…The job. What can I say about the job? No uniform. No company car. No team-building day once in a while. I mean in all the years I've been here…

…And well all those years do you think they mean anything? Like Debenhams bonus points for all the stuff…

…It has to right?

I mean we don't take the job for peace and quiet do we? The good life. I mean we choose to do the job right? We choose it don't we? To feel this well / to feeling…

So… (*Raising her empty glass in the air.*)

(STELLA *drops her raised arm.*)

…Here's to feeling something.

(*Short beat.*
STELLA *steps down off the table.*
STELLA *takes a big mouthful from her wine glass.*)

I mean you feel it don't you? You feel that calling? I know…

…Well I know I have some personal feelings about it. I mean I've seen it from both sides haven't I? That bloody three hundred and sixty degrees that they're always going on about.

I felt it this morning anyway. I bloody felt it. This morning usual thing you know wake up, get Mum up and I'm just getting her breakfast of porridge and / And if she doesn't get her porridge / Don't ask! So off it goes. My mobile on the kitchen table…

(*Short beat.*)

…I answer it. Elayne calling. (*Pointing.*) Yeah you Elayne. To check I'm still doing the last one today. That I hadn't forgotten. That it was in my diary. I say –

Of course I remembered.

…*It's about consistency…*

…*And consistency is important…*

Didn't I? I would never abandon one of mine. Not mine. I mean who would? Who would do that? Leave her there alone. Never. Not me. I'll be there I say. Didn't I? How could I forget? My last one? No way.

(*Short beat.*)

All this wouldn't be worth it if we weren't there for each other. Her waiting there that's what it's about. Not me and my tomorrow…

…I mean tomorrow is another day and tomorrow won't be like this will it? Today and tomorrow are as far apart as winter and summer. And before tomorrow well…

…There's today. So I say –

Just as long as I can still get my hair done!

(STELLA *laughs out loud*.)

Seriously though that new salon has squeezed me in last minute and I want my hair to look nice for tonight.

Tonight's the night! Last chance to see your faces. Last chance to be part of this…

…I don't know what I'm trying to say but it's about getting the job done isn't it? And she's alright. This one. You know what I mean? Something about her makes me hope that she'll make it somehow. That's all I can do now. Hope.

(*Short beat.*)

I usually get there before the vultures but today they're early. And I can see them. The drug dealers. Circling and preying. Even in the morning rain they're there waiting to peddle temptation. Waiting to steal the fucking hope. I shouldn't go on but it makes me so angry. Vultures.

It's a wait but I have Scrabble on my phone. And Radio 2. I hear the gates go and I see her come out. And you can't miss her. Her long legs. Forgot how tall she is. Hands in her pockets and head down. I know it's her by the way she plays with her hair. She always plays with her hair. I jump out the cab and I wave at her. She seems nervous but no more than usual. And I say –

Remember me? I came a couple of weeks ago to talk about what we're going to do today. And the week before that. And a couple of weeks before that too.

Nothing…

…*Remember you said I talk too much?*

That breaks the ice. This is the bit of the job I love. Loved. The human-contact bit, the breaking-the-ice bit. The breaking-into-a-smile bit. And there's that feeling.

The reason why we do it. That thing that makes you wake up every morning to do it.

(*Short beat.*
STELLA *steps down from the table. She sits on the edge of it.*)

The cab drives away from those gates. She looks cold. And she's just sitting there counting the money over and over. Ten pounds, twenty pounds, thirty pounds, forty. Forty-six pounds that's what she gets for making it out. I give her the mobile phone which I've brought for her. With credit. Most jump on it and before long you're listening to non-stop chat with friends, with family, about all sorts…

…But not her. She just stares at it…

…I don't know what she's thinking. But I look out at the rushing world outside the window too and I'm thinking how today and tomorrow are as far apart as winter and summer. And tomorrow…

…That reminds me of something my gran would have said. She was always saying things like that. I remember once she took me to the park. Middle of summer. All the other kids playing. I was holding her knitting. Suddenly she walked us to the edge of the pond in the park. Stood right on the edge of it holding my hand. And I look at her like don't you dare. I'm five and that's what I'm thinking. She looks at me and says –

'*Fear is your worst enemy and your closest friend. Learn to live with it!*'

And just like that she lets go of my hand and jumps in.

(STELLA *cups her mouth with her hands.*)

That was my gran Jan. She definitely needed psychiatric assistance. But see that never left me. Her words. Her honesty…

…And I want to be honest with Joanne. And she looks like the type they might scare so I tell her how it's going to be. First stop probation. And you know what after all these years, and the things I think about the job at least we're not like them. 'The Enforcers.' At least we still have a voice. Not just papers to push about. Riot acts to read. Nothing human about that job now is there? There used to be. Now?…

...I do feel for them. I mean at least I knew I was losing my job. Not an email one morning from some faceless management arsehole from God knows where in the world telling you you've been replaced by a machine. Robot Probation. Like RoboCop without Arnie!! The joys of privatisation eh!

(*She laughs nervously.*)

I get her well prepared and by the time we get to them. It's easy. After ten months inside, she can hardly string a sentence together. She could say it herself but somehow she is silenced by all of this. Lost. Cat not only got her tongue but bloody refused to give it back! But before we leave there I have her saying all the right things. That's what I'm here to do isn't it?

We take their forms, the dos and don'ts, and put a reminder in her phone for the next appointment...

...Anyway I knew we didn't have long before our date with the doctor. You have to get it all sorted before release, before crisis. Referrals have to be booked. And I could see there were problems. Just a girl you know.

(STELLA *is lost in her thoughts for a second.*)

Well you won't believe this. The doctor hands them over and I don't recognise the name of it and neither does she. You know the prescription? And so there she is standing there with a whole two weeks' supply of pills with the wrong name. I should of said something... I should have asked him –

What are they? Are they right?

Give her what she knows.

Who's going to check on her tomorrow? Who's going to make sure they're working for her?

Who cares now?

But I don't say anything. I don't want to worry her. And all said and done this will keep her going until her reassessment. And I mean she promises to take them at the right time, in the right dosage and all I can do is bloody hope so.

From the doctors to Homeless Unit. We're running behind now.
I really don't want to be late. My split ends are desperate. We
wait with our number. Letter in hand. Thought it was sorted.
Pleaded a million ways and you know what they say? –

'No. The best we can get is a hostel.'

I ask –

*You want to put a vulnerable young woman in a wet hostel with
drunks and drug dealers?*

She says –

'We've got no choice.

That's the best we can do.

*She's luckier than some. She could be sleeping on a park bench
and God knows what would happen to her then.'*

I ask to speak to one of the supervisors. And this might sound
wrong but the stress of it is getting to her. And she's playing up.
She's shaking and we're starting to make a scene. They only
ever seem to care when someone is really losing it. She's not
having a breakdown of mega-proportions but the twitching of
the hair is getting worse and it helps and they put her in another
queue to be seen by a housing manager. They can always
authorise something better. Maybe a B&B. But they promise to
take care of her. She has to wait but she'd stopped shaking…

…And I look at my watch. And I look at her sitting there, barely
breathing, clutching the paper bag of pills and the phone,
staring at the bright-red watch on her wrist…

(STELLA *looks round the room. Desperate, tears welling up.*)

…I'm not sure I should but I have to go.

And I am thinking about tomorrow. And I'm thinking how
today and tomorrow are as far apart as winter and summer and
tomorrow who's going to come to save me?…

…But what choice do I have? I can't / She can't / I mean. And I
look at her and I can see me sitting there. First day out. No one
talking to me. Just me and my head, and a Tube map, and sitting
waiting for hours. Alone. But at least I had Mum. She was

always there. And now I'm paying her back aren't I? Now she
has me. My mum...

(STELLA *holds back her tears*.)

And yeah tomorrow I'll feed her, wash her, and sit in the house
with her watching TV all day cuz she's too scared to go out, too
scared to wash her hair, too scared of everything. Me the carer.
The bather. Maybe one day I'll get too scared too and then
what? That's my tomorrow.

(*Short beat.*
STELLA *stands staring out at everyone*.)

But we need each other don't we? They need me and well...

...I didn't know what that feeling was, but now I do. I need this
too because all those Joannes they keep coming out of prison
don't they? And today as I'm walking away, I'm looking at her.
And I'm seeing all this and all the women who leave prison every
day with no one to meet *us / them* through the gate. All those gates
with no friendly face waiting for you. All those vultures. All those
gates with no...

...Well me. And maybe today I saved someone's life.

And tomorrow...

...I'll think about her tomorrow in my new life...

(STELLA *sits at her desk again.*
STELLA *runs her hand over the desk. Caressing.*
She lifts her cup up.)

Here's to me and to you Joanne. We made it through another
day.

(*She runs offstage, sobbing.*

Lights dim.)

GRACE

Ursula Rani Sarma

Character

GRACE

Lights on **GRACE** *standing still, head cocked to the side, listening, trying to catch something or to recall. She's got a nervous energy about her, reined in at first but once we get to 'see me' it breaks free, as if the words are coming tumbling out, almost without her control.*

Accidents. Puzzles. Coincidences. (*Beat.*) This song... you know this song? Something about landscapes... something about accidents and puzzles and coincidences... it's playing somewhere... spilling out of a car window into the rain... this girl is singing. Her voice just soaring up and over all this drudgery... 'All that no one sees, you see, what's inside of me'... (*Beat, this has resonance for her.*) It is beautiful... (*Looks down at her hands, examines them.*) My hands are wet... it's not from the rain... I'm crying... me... (*Beatific smile.*) I'm crying...

(*Beat.*) See me... see me at one. Soft, pliable, gums and smiles, wide awake looking out over the world, brand new. See a million white cotton vests singing on my mum's clothes line. See me in a bouncer, bouncing, see my little pink finger curled around my dad's, grasping his face, the rough beard, the sad laugh lines, the pockmarks, the scars, see me loving him with every cell of my tiny self. (*Beat, she lets the image sit and fade.*)

See me at ten now, with my brother on the clay-tile roof of our house and him saying, 'Listen, if you stand real still and hold your breath, you can hear the sleigh bells.' See me listening, believing, really believing that I could hear them, believing in the magic, see my hand in his, see me loving him so much I think it might burst out of my chest like a Labrador and knock him down. See me looking up there into all that vast inky dark, thinking I could see the light from Rudolph's nose, pulsing like a beacon across the Milky Way. (*Beat, she lets the image sit and fade.*)

See me at fifteen then, grief-struck, throwing some fading flower down into the pit they buried my dad in, looking at my mother sitting there not saying anything, not breathing even, just watching and thinking, there goes my man… See me thinking he hated flowers, they made him sneeze. (*Beat, there's a piercing pain to this, he was her anchor.*)

See me rebelling, smoking, drinking, necking, being a little bitch, craving something I didn't understand. See me in a clique, five of us huddled in a corner wearing black and looking unapproachable, swapping boyfriends, torturing teachers, trying so hard to be cool it hurt. And then stop, wait…

(*Beat, the memory has caught her like a wave of nausea, this is raw, too real, too present.*)

In the classroom, schoolyard, lunch room, there's always one… and she's too tall, too fat, too spotty, too flat, too nerdy, too rich, too poor, too dull, too different… and she's prey for kids like us, in our warm little pack, she's fair game. And I don't remember the beginning, probably name-calling, mocking, taunting, then pinching, poking, prodding, hair-pulling – (*Remembering.*) and then lunchtimes in the chip shop, waiting for her to pass, pelting her with burgers, pickles, curry sauce, Coke cans, and all the time us laughing, laughing at the sheer adrenalin of it… of getting away with it… of the power of it. (*Pause, the memory haunts her.*) And then this… this… see this…

(*Rawer still, open, alive. Maybe the sparkle of a disco ball, faint like a memory, echoes of school-hall music behind.*)

The night she turns up at a school disco in her uniform. We were all ripped jeans, Radiohead, Doc Martens… and here was this kid… just all fucking wrong. So we got Timmy Franklin to ask her to dance and the look on her face, unspeakable delight – (*Suddenly she's this girl, dancing, her arms around Timmy's neck.*) 'He picked me.' She even looked around, she smiled at me… and then once he had her up there two of my gang went up behind her and unzipped her skirt, fell to her ankles, and she just stood there, frozen, long white legs and white granny pants.

(*Long beat, the horror of it, she steps out of the girls skin and away so that she can look at her now from the outside.*)

A teacher stopped the music – (*The music stops but the light continues to sparkle.*) silence, laughter, shrieks of it, great banshee wails of it and still she just stood there and then she looked at me and the force of that, what I saw there, the immensity of it, of what we had done, of what I had let happen, of what I was part of. The injustice of it rising up in my throat like battery acid, that taste, chemical, inhuman, toxic. (*This is the crux of it, what's been eating her ever since.*) And still I did nothing... I did nothing to help.

(*Beat, stops, breathes.*) She hung herself two weeks later, or tried to, but it didn't quite work. Her mother found her, rushed her to the hospital but the damage was done. Cerebral anoxia, her brain had been shut off from oxygen for too long, she basically had a stroke and that was it for her, rest of her life in a wheelchair getting her meals through a straw... and we did that. (*Beat.*) I did that. For a laugh. She was fifteen years old. (*Beat.*)

See me now at nineteen, ditched the clique. See me stacking shelves at tesco, drinking my wages, getting shitty tattoos – (*Pulls up her shirt to reveal a shitty tattoo on her stomach.*) shagging the wrong guy, getting knocked up... (*Beat.*) And I didn't want you at first, but that day in the clinic waiting I just kept thinking of you coiled inside me like a bud, of the drumbeat of your tiny pink heart, how your little finger would curl around mine, thousands of white vests singing brightly on my washing line... and I couldn't part with you.

Then see me at twenty-four living in a shithole with neighbours from *Crimewatch* and nine-year-olds smoking weed in the stairwells and twelve-year-olds pushing prams of their own and I took one look at you, my Lauren, my angel and that was it... I knew I had to do something to change our fate... so I did.

So see me now... police officer with the London Met, small town house, single mum, making ends meet, surviving... and that's me... that's the string of events that led to me. Here. Now.

(*Beat, she cocks her head again, trying to listen, maybe the echo of the song again.*)

You know this song? The thing about it making me cry... is that I don't cry... not since I was fifteen, not since that night in the disco, when something in me just sort of crusted over, and nothing since, not even when my mum died or when you were born. (*Beat. Hopeful now.*) And I know what it was, that thing that the universe saw me do, that it recognised, that it acknowledged… it was tonight…

I'm on with Harry… nice guy decent bloke… believes in doing things by the book, sleeps a sound eight hours knowing he spent his day fighting crime. Anyway, we get this call from a hostel… St Bart's… horrible place… halfway house. It's like honey to the dealers and pimps… they come around selling, recruiting. These girls have nowhere else to go, no family, no friends, easy pickings. Out of prison clean and five hours later they're getting high in the jacks of St Bart's… what else are they going to do?

Tony the hostel manager is waiting for us, he's anxious, chain-smoking, sweat patches on his shirt. It's started to rain but he's still hovering around the doorway. He tells us that some new girl, Joanne, arrived today, claims another girl stole her watch and pills while she was in the shower. 'What kind of watch?' 'Some cheap Micky Mouse plastic piece of shit.' 'And the pills?' 'She's a nutjob, kicking, scratching, biting, she's not right in the head.'

The reception is brown, dark and damp, the wallpaper peeling back on itself in curls, smell of electric heaters evaporating mould thick in the air. Tony gestures to a door. 'I locked her in the kitchen,' he says, 'The other girl is in room five.'

I take the kitchen. Joanne is curled up on a table like a puppy. First thing I notice when she unfolds is she's tall, like really tall, like she's been stretched out, like one of those pale-blue birds you see standing on one leg in a river, still, not moving, watching. And then her eyes, wild and sad, ready to fight, ready to pounce. 'I'm Officer Clancy, I just want to hear your side of the story.'

She's not making sense, words jumbled and scattering, nothing linear, nothing to get a hold of. 'You get out today?' I say, and she looks away. She knows. 'You know what this means,' I say, 'Fighting? For your licence? You're going back inside.' And then suddenly, those eyes are clear, intent, desperate, like a cloud lifting, 'My father gave me that watch when I was ten.' 'And the pills? Medication? For what?' 'They weren't even the right ones, I was on lithium in prison. I told the GP today but she wouldn't listen.' And I can see it now… she's sweating, body is shaking, like a junkie in detox. I think maybe she's lying, maybe she's on heroin and needs a fix. I call her on it... and she just shakes her head, calmly, says 'no', and I believe her. Then silence, and then, 'I don't have anyone.' Just that, simple, clear, weighted like an anchor, 'Do you?' I think of you Lauren, lost in dreams, your arms reaching out for me half-asleep. I ache for you, but to summon you into this place seems all wrong so I say, 'I'm asking the questions here.' She nods, looks away, then back, those big lakes of blue eyes pinned on me, 'Help me.' (*Beat, steps back, head shaking*.) 'I have to report the incident,' I tell her, 'I don't have a choice.' 'Everyone has a choice,' she says and then this... clear as a bell... 'I can't go back.' (*Beat*.)

And suddenly I see her, the moments that have defined her, that have led her to this kitchen tonight, standing in front of me, shaking, saying going back to prison will break her. And again I believe her, I can feel the weight of her whole life in my hands and I am there again... (*The disco ball and music fade up like a distant memory*.) Maybe it's the paleness of her skin or those long limbs trembling that sets that voice in my head going... Do something... just fucking do something... don't let this happen... don't let this happen... this is what you've been waiting for... isn't it?

I tell Harry we'll keep this one between the two of us... and he doesn't like it but I knew he wouldn't... 'We have to follow procedure,' he says, 'Anything happens down the line...' 'Don't you feel sometimes that you have to make a call for yourself? Like you have a say in all this? In what the right thing really is?' He looks at me, doe-eyed. 'We have to report it,' he says. 'No we don't, we fucking don't, all we have to do is what we think is right. And this is the right thing, I'm sure of it, I'm one hundred per cent convinced, all this girl needs is a second chance. Trust me... trust me...'

And then we're back out in the rain heading for the car and my heart's flying, pounding, blood surging in my ears and I can feel it, the lightness of it, like some great beast of a bird that has been nailed to my shoulders all this time has just taken flight. I almost think I can hear it rising up, beating its wings against the sodden air... climbing steadily upwards, its red eyes glinting smaller and smaller, away and up, into the dark...

(*The sound of wings beating the air, moving further and further away. She is still now, released.*)

And then this song… it has taken root somewhere inside me and has bedded down, all the way home it's been coursing through my veins and arteries and cells… and my whole body is humming… singing… released… all the way home to you, now, here, watching you sleep, wanting you to know and understand, wanting you to see… accidents, puzzles, coincidences. 'All that no one sees you see, what's inside of me. Every nerve that hurt you heal, deep inside of me.' (*Beat, smile, proud.*) See me my love… see me…

(GRACE *begins to hum 'Jóga' by Björk. She stops, breathes, her smile is beatific, hypnotic, infectious. Lights down.*)

KATHLEEN

Deborah Bruce

Character

KATHLEEN

KATHLEEN *comes in with a cup of tea, her handbag, a pasta salad in a Tupperware and a neck pillow.*

She puts her stuff down and stands for a moment, arms crossed across her body, tapping rhythmically and lightly on her shoulders. She closes her eyes and breathes steadily. Tapping. She's distracted, stops, looks behind her, then resumes. Faster rhythm, eyes scrunched shut. Bit panicky.

Okay.

And put it down.

Okay. There we are. Let it go.

(*The tapping slows. Gives herself a squeeze, opens her eyes.*

Forces a smile. Stops smiling. Looks at her watch.)

God's sake.

Dear me. Not good, not good. Let it go. Dear me.

Can I stop you there because I have to ask you, politely, not to speak to me like that please. Because I'm halfway through a ten-hour shift and you're not the only person that's come in here tonight needing attention. Okay. So. Please wait your turn. Sit quietly and wait your turn.

(*Tears come.*)

For God's sake Kathleen what are you crying for you stupid woman? He's not the first person to speak to you like that. He won't be the last.

(*Arms crossed, tapping, eyes closed, breathing through the mouth, self-soothing.*)

Let it go put it down let it go, that's right.

(*A mantra.*) What's trivial to us is not trivial to them. When a person lives on their own, they whip themself up into a state.

They're frightened. Say he lives on his own and he hasn't got anyone. Take pity, be kind, find empathy. He's full of fear. You know all this.

(*Opens eyes.*)

Find empathy. Okay.

(*Gathers herself.*)

Good.

(*Starts to deal with pasta salad and finding a fork in her handbag.*)

No need to be so bloody rude. Do you mind? I've been doing this job for twenty-eight years and I'd need to be paid a darn sight more than nine pound an hour to put up with being spoken to like that love. So, y'know. Fuck off.

(*Takes a long breath, breathes out through her mouth.*)

Let it go.

(*She puts her hand on her heart.*)

Pounding!

Give myself a heart attack.

Never mind behind the desk, I'll be on the corridor outside triage lying on a stretcher. Mick'd have to get his own lunch, kitchen like a bomb's hit, lids off everything.

So. Don't want that do we? Get. A. Grip.

(*Eats her pasta salad.*)

Kathleen Parker. You're not the NHS. You can't make decisions on reception, you can't accept responsibility for diagnosis or rejection. Your responsibility is for the welfare of people while they're in the waiting room. You are the face of the NHS, just the face. Not the NHS. The face.

(*Breathing. Tapping. Looks at the clock.*)

Oh Pam, have you got a minute?

Pam, can I have a word with you love? I don't want to mess up the rota. It's just. It's coming up to thirty years you know, on nights, it's. I'm not getting any younger.

Pam. Quick word.

Pam, love. What's the chance of moving on to days? Sorry to ask again, it's just, since the 'change', I don't bounce back like I used to. I can't sleep. I can't shake stuff off. I'm going under.

Listen to me, big drama!

I'll do her an email. Set it all out in an email.

About the panic attacks. Not panic attacks the not sleeping. I'd sleep on a clothes line when I was younger. It's the red-carded ones flashing up on the system every five minutes after the pubs close. You back again? Only one lot of security for the whole yellow wing and me a lone worker it's not right. Back and forth, present three or four times in one night some of them.

Should be asleep now, recharging the batteries – no chance.

The thing is they come in when you're dealing with someone else don't they, and you don't notice them at first and after a while you're like, who's that? They're just sitting there, don't even come up to the desk. And the grid's down after ten-thirty, they don't like that. And you're shouting through the grid, they're pretending they can't hear you. You've got to get up and walk round.

Excuse me! Excuse me! Can I help you?

Yeah, I've got mental-health issues.

Only gets worse when it's raining.

(*Pause.*)

Don't speak to me like that, I'm not a piece of shit on your shoe. I don't make the decisions, I'm not the NHS. I'm a lone worker.

Breathe for Christ's sake Kathleen, you know how to bloody breathe you've done enough courses.

(*She takes time to breathe.*)

Wearing this stress like a corset, I could be in bloody Downton me.

(*Breathe.*)

Look around you. Take the outside in.

(*Breathe.*)

Walls. Floor. Locker. Bin. Ventilation thingy. Hand sanitiser. Table. Chair.

(*Breathe.*)

Satsuma. Gary's fleece.

(*Breathe.*)

Okay. You are part of the world.

That's it, get a grip, not all about you.

Two birthdays coming up this week, two cards to post. So.

Need to get that sorted.

(*Breathe.*)

Pam.

I've had it with nights.

It's a chaos I can't keep my head above.

I imagine myself climbing up on the desk and screaming Help Me! I'm full to the brim of you all. I'm choking on you, I'm gasping for air here people.

One after another, the emergencies that won't be squeezed into the Monday-to-Friday nine-to-five. We're the crisis team, the mental-health team and the police behind that desk and my God they pour through that door, it's the only door they can fit through. Used to go a couple of hours, say, with just the odd one coming in, now there's ambulances in queues and no empty seats the whole shift. And the police bring them here. No consistency, no sharing of information, an answer machine if you're lucky, leave a message if you want but no one's got time to call you back.

I look at these people, who are you?

Their welfare in the waiting room is my responsibility. I'm reading the signs in ten seconds. Starting from the beginning every time. *Groundhog Day* every day.

(*Moves towards us.*)

Out the corner of my eye, I thought it was our Laura. In she comes, I thought, it's our Laura! Please God, let it be our Laura.

Just a young woman. Taller, but the same age as our Laura although she looked like she'd lived a different life, not like she'd been a kid who'd had her school uniform ironed and folded, because I never missed a day doing that, not one, on nights all these years, but I'd come straight in from work, put breakfast on the table with my coat still on. The kids never wore a shirt Wednesday that they'd worn Tuesday. I'd be in for them after school, always did a hot tea. I look at this young woman and I see our Laura, 'Who are you?', in my head that is, only 'How can I help you?' out loud.

She's crying. Proper crying. Tears falling out of her eyes and onto the tell-tale neat white lines on her arms. I say, 'It's alright love, take your time,' and I hand her a tissue and she takes it but she doesn't wipe her face, just holds it. 'What's the problem, how can I help you?' I mean it, I want to help her, that's the bit of the job I hold on to. How can *I* help *you*?

She goes, 'Help me miss, there's nowhere to go miss.'

Always 'miss', it's an easy mistake.

'I'm not going back to the hostel, you can't make me, the men are off their faces, my head's too wrecked, someone's nicked my watch! My hands are numb, the voices shout me down, I'm rattling. Cos they've gave me the wrong meds haven't they? I took them but they're wrong. My heart's bursting, I'm dizzy I'm sick, I'm gasping for air, I'm falling I'm shrinking I can't hear what you're saying it's just echo and hum. I'll kick in a phone box and cut my throat with the glass, I'll rob some scissors and stab myself in the chest. I've made a tourniquet from a plastic glove, you can't take it off me because I haven't done it yet, but I will.

'Section me,' she says, 'I'm a danger to myself and others, I'll do what I have to do, I'll section myself if that's what it takes, just get me a bed.'

Or maybe she says nothing.

I can't think now. Maybe she just stares.

Anyway.

There's a box for suicidal intent, I lift a pen, I tick it.

I say, 'Sit down. I'll get someone to see to you.' My voice is less than I expect it to be.

And I'm thinking, oh if I could just take her home with me. Imagine it. Her sat at the table eating toast, Mick talking about his fishing trip with the pub-quiz pals, her jacket hanging over the radiator, her bag inside the door of our Laura's room. A cup of hot tea, I could heat some soup even, I could be a mum for an hour or two.

Pam! Your face! As if!

I was feeling shaky already if I'm honest. But next up it's him. Pointing his fingers in my face. Through the grid.

He comes right up to the grid, presses his mouth right into it, I can see his teeth all close up. 'What do you care?' he says. Aggressive, proper nasty. 'With ya cuts and ya community plans and ya broken promises.' I can feel the wetness on my chin as his spit sprays onto the face of the NHS and I would say this was the straw that breaks the camel's back but we're full up as it is man, no space in the waiting room for a bloody camel.

The girl who looks like Laura is gone. Slipped out while I deal with this nonsense. I want to call Mick and tell him about her, that's a kind of madness isn't it?

My eyes prickle and burn. I'm tired and flat and I wonder, am I standing here? I can't feel my feet. I'm swaying.

What do you want me to do?

Take them all home? I do! I do! I take them all home most mornings. Buckling under the weight.

I get in, walk past the dishes and the dirty washing, I'm telling you Pam, my standards are slipping. Been weeks since I bothered with the tie-backs on the lounge curtains.

Shower, PJs, lie down. Close my eyes.

They're all there, curled up on the bed next to me, squeezed into the drawers of my bedside cabinet, in my glasses case, wrapped round the legs of the bed.

With their broken toes and high temperatures and domestic incidents and split lips and cracked heads and stomachs needing pumping and hearing voices and handcuffed to police. The schizos and psychos, knives hidden in socks, the boys wanting their mums. Rumbling appendixes and no GP appointments and infected dog bites and third-degree burns, the pub fights and chest pains, the luckless and the poverty struck and the poor lonely live-alones with no one to tell them to take two aspirin and get an early night.

Here they are. Beside me.

All waiting to be seen.

ALICE

Theresa Ikoko

Character

ALICE

Alice is thirty years old. She is the service and operations manager at St Bart's hostel. One of many hostels in the supported housing organisation she has worked for, for the last three years. Alice worked her way up to her position, from senior caseworker. However, the role leaves much to be desired. She is constantly under pressure to make wonders from nothing and to hide/undo the damage caused by an underfunded organisation, in a stretched and pressurised sector, with ineffective ways of working.

Alice is the only child of a Nigerian mother, who is traditional, family-oriented and a devout Catholic. Alice is not these things. Though, she would like to meet someone and settle down. She's not sure how much of those wants are her own, or sprung from seeds planted by her mother and friends, many of whom are on their second child.

Alice is confident. She is energetic. She can be immature. She is youthful. She is incredibly smart and driven. She can be intimidating. Alice talks too fast and, some would say, she thinks too much.

ALICE *huffs. She carries a bucket of cleaning supplies. She is dressed too smartly. The place is filthy. She begins cleaning. She sings to herself as she does.*

She notices something. She digs it out. It is a red child's watch.

You'd be surprised the things we find in here. I say we... but it's really not supposed to be me. I've been climbing the rickety St Bart's career ladder for years, and I'm lower-middle-senior management now. It's got to get done though I suppose. We've got a waiting list a mile long and every day this room sits empty is money down the drain. Tony's off with stress and with the rate these agency staff cost – forget it.

It's got to get done, and someone's got to do it... And I'm usually the 'someone'.

(ALICE *cleans.*)

Tony found a Rolex once. Imagine that? On housing benefit, *still* in rent arrears, I might add... can't afford the weekly three-pound service charge, but there's a Rolex under your bed? Just forgotten – abandoned – like an odd sock. Couldn't make it up. Sounds like something off one of those Channel 5 docs. Cameras following chavs around some unheard part, of the whitest corner, of Black Country. Ellesse tracksuit uniforms, lip piercings from Year 6 up and more ASBOs than healthy teeth.

I had a good mind to pawn it – the Rolex. I didn't. I thought about it. For a second. Maybe five... ten Mississippis, but I gave it to the police. I'm just saying... that *could* have done more for us than it'll do in some forgotten corner of a dusty evidence room... *If* it ever made it there...

Well it's true... We've all thought it. I mean, if I was making peanuts, dodging bullets, budget cuts, and hepatitis-soaked needles, equipped with only pepper spray and a stab-proof vest, I'd be looking for compensation here and there myself.

That officer that come in here the other day, when it all kicked off – who, by the way, is who they really need to sit under the interrogation light. If *she* had just done *her* job – protected her – the girl – from herself…

Anyway, that officer, her, yeah, she definitely needs to start skimming a bit off the top – a few quid here and there when she arrests a drug dealer – she could definitely put the extra money to good use. I assume financial constraints is the reason her hair looked the way it did… And the excess baggage under her eyes… as big as my mum's at Lagos Airport…

Three times the limit clearly stated on the website, Mum's boarding pass, and in bright, red, two-foot writing all over the airport. And if I dare suggest we leave something behind, 'Mum just leave it,' she spits venom, 'Oya, just keep quiet there. Did I ask you? (*Kissing her teeth*.) Id-dyot.' Scowling at me all embarrassed like. *I* should be the one embarrassed – we pack and repack, in the middle of check-in, for an hour. *Every* time. My Agent Provocateur bras smuggling stock fish and my favourite tights stuffed with suya pepper. *This* is why I'm single – fishy nipples and a spicy crotch.

(*Looking at the watch*.) All of this… over *this*? I'd have probably thrown it away if I hadn't read the incident report. '*The* red watch'… A plastic angel of destiny – (*Inspecting the watch*.) made in Hong Kong.

(ALICE *becomes annoyed. She cleans hard*.)

Serious incident *inquiry*. '*Inquiry*' my left bunion. They want me to – (*Stopping cleaninig, raving*.) if you're expecting me to be dignified, to present myself before you, head lowered, and brow furrowed under some false sense of responsibility – if you think I should feel ashamed – responsible… sit here, while you sit there and pretend, while *I* pretend… Let's just call this what it is… (*Scrubbing hard*.) a witch-hunt. A panicked, hysterical search, pitchforks and torches aloft, seeking out '*facts*' and information – Not the *real* stuff though – Not the stuff you've spent years asking me to hide and patting me on the back for magicking away – No, not that. You're searching for evidence that says this is *my* fault, not yours, not ours, just mine. So you can roll it up in me and toss me over the bridge, weighted down by lies, never to be seen again, while you remain blameless and put out an ad in the *Guardian* for your next unsuspecting scapegoat. I will not allow you to burn me at the stake, to cover the stench of *your* neglect and failure…

(ALICE *stops cleaning.*)

That's what I *should* have said… It's not my fault. I… I've made requests… countless – But – (*To herself, chanting.*) 'Bums in beds, bums in beds, bums in beds. Payment by results. Bums in beds. Payments by results. Bums in – '

(*The phone rings, snapping* ALICE *out of the chant. She looks at it, but doesn't answer.*)

Mum. I'm supposed to be on a date. Third one this month. (*In her mum's voice.*) 'Thirty and not married, not engaged, not dating, no viable prospects on the horizon'… She wouldn't say it, but it's pretty much an abomination of biblical proportion – I lie, she does say it – often. Yes, I'm only thirty, but my mum thinks Nigerian years are like dog years. She says marrying me off is more or less impossible – like finding someone to adopt the three-legged, blind dog, with emphysema, from the rescue shelter. My mum looks at me, and I swear she sees the fires of hell engulfing my womb and sealing her fate as the lone grandchild-less one, in her little hymn-singing, salsa-dancing, daily-doctor-visiting, old-lady gang; armed with Bible passages, incoherent sayings and proverbs, and a lack of tact, sharp enough to draw blood.

She once told my friend – Tilly – that she predicted Tilly's child was to be a girl, because girl fetuses make their expectant mothers ugly. To her face. She said this to Tilly's face. At her baby shower. In an *unsolicited* toast-slash-prayer, in front of sixty guests.

(*The phone rings again.*)

Uncle Ike's sister-in-law's cousin's wife's nephew's colleague – my date… the more degrees of separation… the more desperate people have become.

There was a pastor's son's schoolfriend – he was grabby. 'Nope, not my hand... that's definitely not my hand Kunle... please, thank you.' The tailor's neighbour – he '*forgot*' his wallet. 'How much?! (*Through gritted teeth*.) Yep. Lobster. Expensive stuff. Worth it? I'm sure. Allergic to shellfish, so I wouldn't know. Nope that's fine. Glad you enjoyed it.' I had to bring in home-made sandwiches for lunch. For a month. There's been countless... There's even been a... a *Jamaican*. He was half – that's how mum sold it – to herself, not me, I'm open to whatever – but that must have been tough for her... like selling her soul to the devil for the promise of grandkids – And yes, in this analogy, Jamaicans, aka – (*In her mum's voice.*) '*Jamos*', are the devil.

Kids... Gosh, the plans I had... The plans we all have... (*Looking at the watch*.) the plans she must have had...

I saw her. I was on my way out as she was on her way in. She stood in the doorway like an overgrown baby, clutching onto sheets of paper, and a bag that I recognised from the pharmacy down the road, as if it were a baby blanket and a handwritten letter, detailing a mother's apology, and dreams and wishes for a better life for the child she is leaving on our doorstep. And this watch, I remember it now, this watch halfway down her skinny little arm, as if a forget-me-not, a keepsake with intentions to remember a mother, who would one day return and reclaim her child.

But these aren't their mothers, the ones who come here. Their mothers don't come for them... not even when... not even now. That box, of her stuff, has been down there, and we've called and we've left messages and no one calls back. No one comes to collect their things... even when it's all that is left of them, in this world. These are *their* mothers. Their mothers are mothers to mistakes and forgotten morning-after pills, conceived, without fathers, bent over the bins, behind M&S, with knickers pushed to the side, while eating a kebab, with semen dripping down their legs and the smell of piss in the air.

Maybe that's what I've got to do to get laid. Hang around behind the M&S on the high street, with a large doner, and no knickers on.

She was tall as well. Really tall. That's maybe why I noticed
her. It's like a secret, sympathetic… No. Supremacist society.
Because deep down, us tall girls know we're better than
everyone else, and 'No I will not help you reach the top shelf in
Tesco, because I can tell, from the look in your eyes, that you
bullied a fellow tall girl in primary school, and now our plan to
exact revenge and silently laugh, while you jump and stretch,
next to a wet-floor sign, is well in progress'… 'I don't care that
you're eighty-three, Betty, you should have thought about that
when you were picking on Long Tall Sally in Year 4. Get your
own Bounty kitchen rolls'… Us tall girls – not the ones that
look like Topshop ads – not the ones that look like that Jenner
girl – they're our arch-nemeses – us *other* tall girls – like the
tall Kardashian – we are a secret, sympathetic, slash
supremacist society… So we see each other, when no one else
does, and we remember each other, in case no one else does,
and our eyes say 'you go girl! You tall beautiful girl! You go.'
So I remember her.

And I remember being the tallest kid in school. Lanky and
awkward and not quite able to cross my legs and tuck them
under the bench as neatly as Kassie in Year 11 – You know the
benches you get upgraded to, the ones you wait four years to sit
on, because they, in your mind are the throne of adulthood, that
come with a wind machine and a soft focus, American, nineties,
soap-opera filter. There's this constant longing and self-
prophesying that one day, when you get to those benches, it will
all fit – your bra, the butt of your jeans, your thoughts, your
place in this world…

I saw her. And her being so young, being all tall and awkward
like that… not quite fitting in her clothes and in her skin – not
quite fitting in this place… in any place…

I knew she wouldn't fit. I *said* she wouldn't… To myself, but I
said it… I think.

That's sort of the problem. There's not enough places for people
in the world to fit into any more. There's not enough funding
they say, and there's not enough evidence and there's not
enough *need*… apparently.

(ALICE *cleans/tidies for a moment.*)

But there *is evidence* – (*Clutching the watch*.) if you want it, there's evidence. Evidence that *this* is failing. Evidence that is bursting out of all the places I've been hiding it for the last three years. Hidden in statistics, in case studies, in rent arrears, in staff sick days, in my head, in the bathroom mould, broken furniture, in the pains in my neck and shoulders, in the one-ply toilet tissue, in staff assaults, in incident reports, in my acne breakouts, in nine-nine-nine calls, in prison recalls, in my occasional stress-induced yeast infection, and in my lack of – (*In her mum's voice*.) 'potential prospects'. And the *need…* the need is blinding, deafening, the smell of it hits the back of my throat on my way to work and makes me gag, it assaults and is assaulted, and I hold my phone with both hands, as I walk from the station, in case it tries to steal it.

(*Pause*.)

The evidence. The need. It is found, cold and rigoured, face-down on the concrete, drowned in her own vomit, the residue of some pill, she probably couldn't pronounce, coating her teeth, with a tan outline where this watch was supposed to be.

And I knew she wasn't supposed to be here. And I said it… in my head… I think.

(ALICE *cleans. Silently, for a moment*.)

LSE, with a first-class and a MBA from King's. Hands and knees scrubbing a floor. Who would have thought? Mum probably… she would have thought. My mother. She definitely would have thought. Maybe she was right, I should have been a lawyer – a banker… *anything* else… but there are just never enough places for people to fit.

BECKY

Laura Lomas

Character

BECKY

Lights up on **BECKY***, her feet are muddy. It's early morning, before dawn. Throughout the monologue, the stage very gradually fills with light as morning breaks.*

You know what I miss most about being a kid? You know what it is? The feeling that like, anything is possible. The feeling that you can be whatever you want, you know?

Used to want to be an astronaut. How mad's that? Can you imagine it?

You know, like you'd just bump into me. Tesco. Fruit-and-veg aisle – be like, 'Alright Becky, haven't seen you in a while,' and I'd just be like, 'Yeah, I know. I've been in space.'

(*Beat.*)

Used to want to be all sorts of things. Footballer. Professional, obviously.

That was sort of my tomboy phase.

Hairdresser. Detective. Vet.

(*Beat.*)

Don't know when I decided to be a teacher. It was just sort of… what happened.

My dad was a teacher. Maybe that was it. They say that, don't they? Stuff like that, runs in families. Didn't have any astronauts in my family so I guess that was a contributing factor.

(*Pause.*)

I went for a… walk.

It's not something I'd normally do. Four in the morning, but…

I couldn't sleep.

I was lying there. David's breath on the pillow next to me.

Carla's words bouncing round the room

Felt like I'd swallowed a stone.

(*Beat*.)

Got in the car and drove out past the station, didn't take me long.

It was weird – different and the same, like how things can be.

Same graffiti on the bridge, weeds coming up through the gaps in the concrete.

The River.

Was like I could see myself, five years ago, skinny arms and scraped-back hair.

Ghost of me.

Sat for a while, just on the steps, watching the water rush out over the weir. Funny feeling. And I know how this sounds but for a while I felt like the river was talking, and for a while it felt like it was saying her name.

(*Beat*.)

It got cold. All the skin on my arms all prickled but still just sat there.

Thought about my first term at Fairmount, my dad happy cuz it was a 'Good school. Nice kids. Good rep.' Said, 'You'll be alright there, Becky. You'll do fine.'

I was terrified. Third day in and I'm taking a group of thirty Year 11s on a trip to some space centre, out in God knows where. I'm at the top of this massive coach, chaos everywhere, the kids just pulling at one another, the fucking hormones in them, honest to God you could smell them

and then I see her.

Joanne.

She's sat in the third row, next to Carla, but she's in her own head, the sun just spilling out across her face. Sort of amber.

And she's reading.

Her lips are going, but just quietly to herself, like a whisper,
or a prayer.

Something.

(*Pause.*)

She wanted to be a scientist.

That's what she'd say. And maybe you're thinking course she
did, kids always say that stuff, but with Joanne it was different.

She had this mind, this mind that was so…

Used to worry that she was bored, that I was boring her, that the
lesson wasn't enough for her, or she already knew it, and I'd
catch her not concentrating, fiddling with her pen in her own
head and then almost out of nowhere she'd just come out with
something.
Just one
sentence, one thought, and the quality of it – you know, the way
her mind worked…

It floored me.

(*Pause.*)

I got up. Felt like the rush of the water over the weir was getting
louder. Thoughts bashing round my head. Things I should have
asked Carla – like 'When?' or or 'Who told you?' or you know

'How did it get so bad?'

My dad told me this thing, when I first started teaching, he said
– and he's not normally like this, but he looked at me and he
goes, 'It ain't easy Becky. They tell you all this stuff in the
training, but that's not even half of it.' He said, 'The real thing
is knowing what's right, and what's best. And the difference
between the two. They can't teach you that.'

I'd forgotten he'd ever said that. It wasn't until later, when I
heard that she'd fallen out with Carla, left home, moved in with
some bloke, older guy from the Chappel Estate, that it came
back to me.

(*Beat.*)

I carried on up the river. Still dark, street lights reflecting off the water. Air felt very still. Too still. Like I was the only thing in motion in the whole world. Like if I stopped then everything might. The river.
Time.

I kept moving. Smoked two cigarettes back to back. Thought about Carla. That she'd come, that she'd even thought to come, to tell me.

Thought that, that was nice.

Thought about how grown-up she looked. Stood there outside the school gates, car keys in her hand. The nuance of it, way she held herself.

I remember them – the both of them, sitting at the back.

Her and Jo.

Sharing a pair of headphones, listening to music on one of their phones. Singing. That song, that song, they loved. Jo belting it, top of her voice.

(*She sings 'Jóga' by Björk*.)

She was so alive, you know? Like too alive, too much. Wanted everything, more than the world had to offer.

(*Pause*.)

I don't know how long it'd been going on for. It could have been a long time. Jo's dad had died when she was thirteen, and it was just her and her mum at home. I only met her the once, that day she came in to talk about what had happened.

I remember them sitting there, other side of this table. Jo with her head down, not looking up, just sitting there flicking the strap of this watch… Mickey Mouse or something. And me playing the part, telling myself it's the right thing – I was doing the right thing. Her mum had to know.

She was different to how I expected. Colder somehow. Sort of woman who could make an art out of washing and ironing a uniform, but couldn't for the life of her, hold a conversation with her own child.

I remember the way she inhaled – little short breaths.

She didn't know what to do with Jo that was for sure. They were two points of a constellation, miles apart and nothing to connect them now that he'd gone.

Or at least that's how it seemed, felt. At the time.

And maybe I should have done something more, and it's not an excuse but it was my second year of teaching and honest to God, if I could get through the day without shaking from too much coffee and too little sleep, then that was probably enough for me.

(*Beat.*)

It was baking. One of them days where the air feels hot to swallow. Kids were like flies inside a jar. I remember I was wearing this pencil skirt, narrow, right down to my knees, I could hardly move in it.

I'd taken them out, the whole class. Walked them the back way, past the station. There was a row of trees halfway along the riverbank, I thought we could sit out there, in the shade a while.

(*Beat. She hesitates.*)

It should have been obvious. She'd been wearing that jumper all week and I swear to God in that heat…

I didn't even think, we were halfway up the river and I turn round and the sweat on her forehead and cheeks, and I just stop, and in front of the whole class go, 'What are you doing, Jo? Take your jumper off for God's sake.'

There was a pause, just a moment.

'I'm alright,' she goes.

But she's not.

'You look like you're gonna pass out'

'I'm fine'

'You don't look fine'

'Well I am'

'It's boiling.'

'I'm not even hot'

'So why are you sweating, Jo?'

(*Beat.*)

There was a look. Strange look. I remember it, she swallowed.

And everyone's waiting for her. They're stood there waiting.

And so she does it.
Slowly, lifts off her jumper.

And she stands there, short-sleeved T-shirt, face burning, and
the marks on her.
these
huge
deep purple cuts. All down, both arms.

(*Beat.*)

She just goes. She's like a bullet, up the river, and I'm running
up there after her, these stupid heels on me, and she's gone, past
the old boathouse, beneath the overpass, out the other side and
there's this shed   one of them power ones, you know? Where
they keep the mains and I can't see her, but I know she's there
cuz I can hear this sound. Like a wheezing, or gulping and I get
around, right round the other side

And I see her.

She's sort of crumpled down next to the wall.

All the air gone out of her,

Heaving, her chest going these big aching sobs.

Graze across her knuckles from where she's smacked the wall.

And the marks, deep purple and angry on her arms.

And I kneel down, right next to her – my fucking pencil skirt,
and I put my hands on her and say 'Jo.' That's it. Just 'Jo.'
Over and over.

But she won't look at me.

She won't look at me.

She won't…

(*Beat.*)

Carla said they reckon she was alone when she did it. Found her
in a park near the hospital, the bottle of pills emptied out next to
her body. Said she'd gone to A and E and they'd turned her away.

(*Beat.*)

It was getting light, but I just carried on up the river. Nowhere
to go, 'cept just to stay in motion for a while. Thinking. All
these ghosts we carry. Like in our bones.

When I reached the overpass, I took my shoes off and stood on
the bank with my feet in the mud. Light was turning, that sort of
blue you get at that time. It was quiet, peaceful in a way that
made me feel very still.

And there was this bird. I think a heron actually, huge, and the
way it lifted up, out of the reeds… like it could levitate. You
know? Like that was a thing, so sort of effortless.

And just for a moment, I had this feeling that maybe the world
isn't that hard a place to be. And I know how that sounds, cuz of
course it is. But then I got to thinking, 'bout this thing my
Grandma used to tell me,
about souls,
'bout how there's only one, like one universal soul for all things
on earth, which is why we have to look after it, cuz everything,
like trees and plants and mountains and rivers and animals
and people. All people.

How we're just one soul.

It sounds stupid when you say it out loud, and maybe it is, but
something about it – about standing there, at five in the
morning…

I understood it.
And I liked it. The thought.

It made sense to me.

The room has now filled with light. 'Jóga' by Björk plays.

A Nick Hern Book

Joanne first published in Great Britain in 2015 as a paperback original by Nick Hern Books Limited, The Glasshouse, 49a Goldhawk Road, London W12 8QP, in association with Clean Break

Stella copyright © 2015 Chino Odimba
Grace copyright © 2015 Ursula Rani Sarma
Kathleen copyright © 2015 Deborah Bruce
Alice copyright © 2015 Theresa Ikoko
Becky copyright © 2015 Laura Lomas

The authors have asserted their moral rights

Cover artist: Ed Fairburn

Designed and typeset by Nick Hern Books, London
Printed and bound in Great Britain by Mimeo Ltd, Huntingdon, Cambridgeshire PE29 6XX

A CIP catalogue record for this book is available from the British Library

ISBN 978 1 84842 544 6

CAUTION All rights whatsoever in these plays are strictly reserved. Requests to reproduce the texts in whole or in part should be addressed to the publisher.

Amateur Performing Rights Applications for performance, including readings and excerpts, by amateurs in the English language throughout the world should be addressed to the Performing Rights Manager, Nick Hern Books, The Glasshouse, 49a Goldhawk Road, London W12 8QP, *tel* +44 (0)20 8749 4953, *email* rights@nickhernbooks.co.uk, except as follows:

Australia: Dominie Drama, 8 Cross Street, Brookvale 2100, *tel* (2) 9938 8686 *fax* (2) 9938 8695, *email* drama@dominie.com.au

New Zealand: Play Bureau, PO Box 9013, St Clair, Dunedin 9047, *tel* (3) 455 9959, *email* info@playbureau.com

South Africa: DALRO (pty) Ltd, PO Box 31627, 2017 Braamfontein, *tel* (11) 712 8000, *fax* (11) 403 9094, *email* theatricals@dalro.co.za

Professional Performing Rights Applications for performance by professionals in any medium throughout the world, should be addressed, in the first instance, to the Performing Rights Manager, Nick Hern Books, The Glasshouse, 49a Goldhawk Road, London W12 8QP, *tel* +44 (0)20 8749 4953, or *email* rights@nickhernbooks.co.uk for details of individual agents.

No performance of any kind may be given unless a licence has been obtained. Applications should be made before rehearsals begin. Publication of these plays does not necessarily indicate their availability for amateur performance.

Woodland
CARBON
www.woodlandcarbon.co.uk
NICK HERN BOOKS
Printed on Carbon Captured paper